Telling the Difference

Telling
the
Difference

Poems by

Paul Watsky

il piccolo editions
by

fisher king press

il piccolo editions by Fisher King Press
www.fisherkingpress.com
info@fisherkingpress.com
1-800-228-9316 Toll free Canada & the U.S.
+1-831-238-7799 International

Telling the Difference
Copyright © 2010 Paul Watsky
ISBN 978-1-926715-00-1
First Edition

Published simultaneously in Canada and the United States of America. For information on obtaining permission for use of material from this work, please submit a written request to:

permissions@fisherkingpress.com

Acknowledgments

I'm grateful to the following publications in which versions of these poems have appeared:

Alabama Literary Review: "Hell Hath No Windows"; *Cathexis*: "For Y: Worry-Free Day"; *Cave Wall*: "The Annual So-Called Hunting Trip"; *Confrontation* (forthcoming): "The Magnificent Goldstein"; *Convolvulus*: "End Games 1"; *Elysian Fields Quarterly*: "Ballplayer"; *Groundwater*: "Twins Discuss Heaven"; *Gumball Poetry*: "My Grandpa, Susan's Grandpa"; *The Noe Valley Voice*: "Piglet Mind"; *Noon*: "For Zoe"; *Oranges & Sardines*: "The Closest"; *Pemmican*: "April, 2003: It's All Over But," "The Girl with the Leash"; *Poetry Flash*: "Busman's Holiday, Cloudy"; *Review Americana*: "What People Earn"; *Snow Monkey*: "For X: Res Casino Weekend"; tel-let (chapbook, *More Questions Than Answers, 2001*): "Relative Unknowns," "Formerly Candlestick Park," " Big Museum," "All Good Things," "Sleepover at the Old House"; *The Distillery*: "Thruway Blizzards, 1968-9"; *The Pinch*: "Cumbersome"; *The Rogue Scholars*: "Temple of Kali"; *The San Francisco Psychologist*: "Toad Fever."

Grateful also to the following people for their invaluable readings of the manuscript: Roger Weingarten, Elizabeth Chapman, Joan Houlihan and the Colrain Conference, Jill Rosser, and Susan Thackrey.

Grateful for the unflagging encouragement of: Jules Burstein, Lynn Franco, Mary Harper, Nancy Kangas, Nancy Keane, Kit Kennedy, Joanne Kyger, Eunice Panetta, Clare Rossini, Scot Siegel.

Grateful to my wife and sons—Clare, Simon, and George— especially for putting up with what poetry puts people through.

Contents

PROLOGUE   xiii

    All Good Things   1

I TEMPLE OF KALI   3

    Cumbersome   5

    Toad Fever   6

    The Magnificent Goldstein   8

    My Grandpa/Susan's Grandpa   11

    Traditional Eats   12

    End Games   14

    Temple Of Kali   16

    Dreaming I'll Love You Dead   21

    Were God A Psychologist: The Afterlife   23

II THE CLOSEST   25

    Sleepover At The Old House   27

    Of Good Extraction   28

    The Closest   29

    Big Museum   31

    Irish Landscape With Spouse   35

    Hell Hath No Windows   36

    Thruway Blizzards, 1968-9   38

    Formerly Candlestick Park   41

    Ballplayer   43

    Daybreak, New Year's, 1993   46

III WHAT PEOPLE EARN   49

   "What People Earn"   51

   Stakes   53

   Who Knows   54

   The Annual So-Called "Hunting Trip"   55

   April 2003: It's All Over But   57

   The Girl With The Leash   58

   Busman's Holiday, Cloudy   60

IV PIGLET MIND   63

   Romances   65

   Becube   68

   Language Fallen Into The Wrong Hands   69

   Upon Encountering Ovid's No Lyres For

      This Lot, No Poetry   70

   Relative Unknowns   71

   Consolation   74

   Rural Diptych   75

   Piglet Mind   77

EPILOGUE   79

   Twins Discuss Heaven   81

For Clare, Simon, George

Prologue

All Good Things

Like the dummy nipple proffered
between feedings, *all good things*
must come to an end palms itself off
as consolation. Just imagine, Feynman
suggests, the universe: expanding
almost eternally so farlong
into who knows where, then—whoomph—
snapping back out of whatever until
creation encompasses less
than a cantaloupe. Feeling reassured,

empowered? If so, you're ahead
of George, wakeful one school night
shortly before his tenth birthday, anticipating
(ingrained habit, crib era,
circa age two) death: his, mine,
his mother's—both the slow, with its bleak
precursors, and the swift, stunning bafflement
of possibility. Nostalgic, he bemoans
everything transitory, including the spirit
of our long-gone diapering games.
I reverse-scroll myself fifty years to when
a middle-aged uncle washed my socks in the bathroom
sink while I rode the toilet seat, laughing to see him
accidentally-on-purpose knock
the wrung out ones back into dirty
water. Now with George sobbing

beside me in the spare bedroom crammed
full of history and poetry books, I bleat
simple-mindedly about conservation of matter,
how wonderful that nothing's unrecyclably lost.
No sale. Desperate, I declaim
a medley of Erasmus Darwin's non-morbid
lousy verse, figuring if the bathos can't jolly him up,
the dullness makes him woozy, and then
I can redeposit George where Simon, his twin, sleeps
tight in orthodontic headgear, where the pet snake waits
buried under its water dish to shed,
and the chartreuse
alarm clock display
illuminates time.

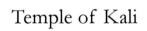

Temple of Kali

Cumbersome

Crayfish out of water—doomed
undoubtedly by going missing
from my son's bedroom aquarium, crawled

out somehow, desperate, and willing
to perish escaping the name imposed
by an observant six-year-old

boy still mourning a week later
when Cumbersome, all tarted up
with dust bunnies, crept forth

from the refrigerator's drip-pan
netherworld, having eluded
kitty Laverne, and mini-Marco

Polo'd, trekking a long hall's
distance to the stairs, clawing
and bouncing down one flight,

retracing half-a-houselength,
then navigating the linoleum's
slippery expanse. Astonishing

and understated all at once,
he couldn't roam again. Never uttering
an audible word, Cumbersome wrote

his true name large. And died
a crustacean Methuselah,
with a weighted screen above his head.

Toad Fever

No one at first believed Bluejay, even though
sometimes he told the truth. It felt better
to say *sure, right, BS, sez you!* than sort out
details garbled by bird-to-bird transmission,
details even more implausible than his elephant
fiasco: *a huge floppy-eared monster with a strangled
snake for a nose*, he jibbered, a snake where
an inquisitive mouse had got stuck. For that
nonsense we laughed him out of our neighborhood,
and for a few months it was nice and quiet.

This time around, if we'd listened we might
have laid in vaccine or lined up hospital beds, but
when he started shrieking about what he called a *cheater*,
an impossibly fast animal that broke out
in spots and stripes and rolled over dead,
we just smirked. *Not a laughing matter*, he sputtered,
it's headed our way, which made him so much funnier—until
Mountain Lion Joe, stiff as a board, turned up
covered with the kind of blotches a confused bird
might call stripes. *That's toad fever!* hollered the jay.

Several charitable animals who reminded us of Joe's
hard luck speculated the marks could have once
been tattoos. Others blamed his lifestyle, insinuated
he did things to deer and sheep before eating them, wondered
if he ever worked toad into his appetite. Uncooperative,
the toads argued they still hadn't lived down the Egyptian
mess and could do without fresh scandals. These toads,
tight-lipped most of the time anyway, dreaded
scientific research, quarantines, witch hunts. *Tough,*
snarled Bluejay, *we've all got things to worry about.*

The Magnificent Goldstein

totters toward the spotlit
circle where a card table supports
three walnuts lined up
inches apart. While the crowd quiets
Goldstein, the finale, looking ancient
in a baggy suit, meditates
briefly, then unzips, brings forth his substantial
organ, and wham wham wham with that
many blows shatters
the hapless fruit. Hysterical
applause from the house. It's some job

telling this story. I could use a little
intelligent help. First-off
the disclaimer: Mostly my material isn't
100% original. So what? Neither was
Shakespeare's. Second, full disclosure:
This whole goddamn thing's a joke I
started in the middle, as a grabber.
I've got no real excuse for jerking you
around. Deal with it. One day I'm putting

together a reading, and thinking how I'm
a guy who enjoys a laugh, especially
at someone else's expense, when
a pal e-mails me an anonymous
gag, the writing so-so at best but the concept—head
and shoulders above his usual
rancid spam. Tweak
the verbiage I can make a double

killing, as I elevate the literary canon
and massage you, dear reader, who

like Everyman, loves a classic
set-up: Travelling salesman at loose ends
in jerkwater town. Eyes circus poster.
Detests circuses. Gets hooked anyway
with one cryptic line:
Don't miss The Magnificent Goldstein!
So he suffers dozens of rotten acts
until that last astounding
performance. Twenty years later his car,
broken down on the interstate, gets towed
to this same decaying burg, and voila!

Goldstein as if he never left. I need
another disclaimer: Goldstein's punchline
may be in dialect but the gag's
not anti-Semitic, rather an allegorical
attempt to intimidate Israel's enemies, though
for such a purpose three targets
seem too few. This time around

an older—if that's possible—slower-moving,
doddery Goldstein faces off against
a trio of wicked coconuts.
Long pause.... Blam
Blam Blam, same as before, they're
vaporized. Overwhelmed,
and aflame with curiosity, salesman seeks
interview. Prodigy admits him

to shabby caravan. *Sir, why switch*
to coconuts? asks the awed visitor. *Vell*
you know, replies our virtuoso, *I'm not such*
a young man any more, and my eyes,
they ain't vhat they used to be. Da Da!

Thanks, kind Thalia. That said,
this treatment still needs to have a suitable
ending—you should pardon
the expression—hammered out. Hope

will be the message!
for America's aging population. Hope
for the gene pool. Upon retirement, Goldstein
plans to donate sperm to a Lithuanian bank. Hope
for the once-alienated salesman, who discovered
a vocation worthy his respect. Hope for walnuts—
permanently off the endangered list. Hope for coconuts—
finally receiving the attention they deserve.

My Grandpa
New York and Miami

Of her eleven kids, his mother
liked him least, marking
the guy as utterly
expendable. Yet nothing
until he hit 96 and stopped
caring could finish off
that mean, selfish, five-foot
shit—not cigar rolling or the bellicose
Irishmen he beat up
in his Hell's Kitchen
deli, not abusing his
wife, not my father's hatred, not
rye whiskey, smokes, gobs of
chicken fat mashed with fried
onions, his stinginess,
greed, or pinochle.

Maybe he convalesced with
interludes when he sat
beneath his prize oil
painting, big as himself,
an old copy. Zeus
in eagle guise, perching
on Hebe's arm. Dulled
varnish didn't hide her frontal
half-nakedness, more soothing
to the eye than his obese
second mrs., who called crappers
the terlet. My stay-at-home
uncles, raised
to be passive, pig-
ignorant countermen, handed
the pre-nup over
to Stepmama. She
disappeared with Grand-
pa's million bucks.
Zeus & Hebe, too.

Susan's Grandpa
Kansas

No plump raccoon tail for the antenna
of his coffin, he drove
a funereal Buick fifty years
right into the ground.

11

Traditional Eats

At ninety-eight, Mother,
sick of assisted-

living food—
their plates always look

the same—still plays
the angles, claims

I miss chopped
liver. So she's giving

the recipe and I can
bring her what little

bit's left over, after
I taste membrane,

and gristle,
slathered with bitter muck.

No more
meat grinder,

remember?
It got left back East.

Tongue they'd seethe.
Calf's liver, broiled,

Dad cranked squelching
through the galvanized

works, along with
fried onions and too

few optional hard
boiled eggs. But

the tongue's tip cold
was nice on sandwiches.

End Games

1.

Grubbing up tough
little weeds,
Mother remarks, *Overgrown*
grass around a tree trunk
is ugly as the hair sticking
out of an old man's
nose. But after

our visit she tells me
when my son and I left she tried
finding us, knowing better but,
as if dazed, repeatedly checking
one or the other
of her rooms.

2.

My aunt's shallow breathing—her
broken ribs, an encore to August's
cracked pelvis. Always slight, now
shrunken, she never says osteo-
porosis, instead that she's like
reconstituted soft cheese, with over-

worked feet from the handkerchief
counter. Into her deafness I shout
questions: pain-free, isn't really
asleep when she shuts her eyes, rejoices
the swelling departed her girlish
legs again at almost 90. Loves

food, sees fine, misses New York, where
her blinds were permanently shut. She
easily ignores the mountain peeping
in her hospital window, a big dirtpile wasted.
I have no conversation, she says, *no
complaints,* kissing my hand hungrily.

Temple of Kali

Natural World

If you're easily bored
or need a parable, I recommend
driver ants, called
siafu in Tanzania, called
Africa's foremost predators
on TV, where they can be seen pouring
twenty-million strong upward
from the ground complete
with sound effects, the chattering
clicks of a stream
in spate, a freshet of wood
fragments and nails, hurrying
themselves along channels formed
by their own scent, hurrying
to the meat market
with a short list: FLESH
of the beetle, the poison-spined
caterpillar, mixed worms,
assorted reptiles, chickens
when available, seasonal rodents
and large mammals, choice
human babies, the fortuitous
drunk passed out
in the wrong place, Granny
when she falls and can't
get up. A wet-
weather phenomenon, they strip

the field of pests, and only
occasionally of the Masai
gardener, too. The siafu,
industrious, self-effacing,
taketh away, taketh away
ugly-style, swarming
into our lungs, clicking chips,
nails, a river of hard
water carrying us off,
down, back home below.

Their Teachings: hang babies
out of harm's way; don't
save your heavy boozing
for Tanzania; when Grandma falls,
keep an eye on her.

2.

Laundry Session, Sunday, 63rd Birthday, VT College
Writers Conference

Small load. I'm estimating
like a dumbass, *The end's
not so close*. But
a buddy in his 50's,

last week: two
strokes—cerebellum,
parietal lobe. Nobody can tell
him why they came

out of nowhere. People here
shared out just enough
quarters for my machines. I sit
in this dorm room, hopeful

I didn't over-lavish cadged dish soap
on my only jeans. Centuries
back, by a river, Issa,
the haiku guy, tuned in

to bugs floating past
on a branch. *Still singing*,
he remarked of them. Good
man, that. Died young.

3.

Bon Voyage Party

My friend, you're dead, late
fifties. The big C. Showed up
three years ago—cervical,
advanced, and from cutting
to new age wholistic whatever, nothing
did the trick.

You licketysplit self-
created as dragon,
star, (mediocre) poet,
exponent of love,
transitioned
into coma without the slightest
hint you were vanishing
headfirst down
the gullet
of a giant
crocodile.

          This
is your memorial
service bedizened with
harping, evangelical
harranguing. Despite
Rumi, Hafiz in English
platitudes, I will stay for the inept
drumming, officious mourners, stay
though only women
who liked you better fat

will speak. Stay to be
assured the body
alone expires, that ectoplasmic now
you travel cheaper, lucky
lucky you. I will stay
until the end when, all grief-
struck, everyone's urged
to choose a polished stone
of yours—one
apiece—and at the exit required
to drop it in a ritual
pot of water—adios
goodbye—for repossession
by your executors.

I wind up left alone
on the patio with *nada*
tangible, *nada* keeping
me company except
ice tea, lemonade, and
an Irish barman grim,
resigned.

      —Next time
she dies, says I,
I'll bring a flask.
—I'll pour, says he.
We nod.

Dreaming I'll Love You Dead

avatar
of high-school friendship, dead
second year at Sarah
Lawrence so long now
there's no good
reason any more
even after a drunk
to dream you
over: A comfortable down-
at-the-heels house and maybe
grad students. Every-
body listens to me even
you sexy small woman
with the heavy braid tight
jeans and snug long-
sleeved sweater
close enough
for your body heft
texture of wool
pearl buttons neck to navel.
We're standing
together in dry
grass exotic
thorn trees scattered on
hillsides down which burst
big game
animals—lions giraffes
stampeding rhinoceros

antelopes many
on fire and crazed
no doubt
about the flames but
there's little smoke.
Why am I not crushed
the hot
hides' thunder
brushing past?

Were God a Psychologist: The Afterlife

you enter a nondescript
office metal
desk two or three straight
backed chairs and sort
pictures into categories you pick
up the naked woman
in chains her bottom
lashed by dwarfs sporting hefty
erections and set it
on the like dislike or neutral
pile cards for all kinds
of moods situations people
resembling your
parents the battle
of Kursk
representative foods
pretty soon you assume
these heaps determine
your placement your permanent
future you intuit where
you're heading and turn
despondent or giddily cheerful
as you sort everlasting cards
day after day
while behind the mirror something
silent
scratches notes

The Closest

Sleepover at the Old House

I don't know where she came from
originally, maybe the South Pacific,
this little flying sex goddess
about eighteen inches long
hanging from a ceiling hook
by string.

       She's very pale, with gold-
accented green wings, nice bare
breasts, pixieish ears, arms
spread and reaching to hug
me. Even though part of her foot's
broken off

       she's heading
up the bed in my direction but angled
to miss my face and sail
out the window, taking her flower-
ornamented black hair, lipstick,
sarong and bangles to
someone more deserving.

       Religion works
that way, makes
me think there's a profound
reason
I'm alone.

Of Good Extraction

Their sleeping quarters engrossed me
when I was four: a lavish
view past those twin
beds to Dad's lab bench rife
with drawers. On top, his inlay
kiln, buffing engine,
and dungeon-master's tools,
overshadowed by a morgue: impressions
shelved in precision rows—grimacing
white plaster maladapted mouths. Best
was his jumbled mayonnaise jar
charnel house harboring
bloodied teeth chosen
neither from brilliance nor deformity;
diseased incisors, swordlike, plunged
haphazardly among root-
gnarled molars, saved
exclusively for gold, their failed
prostheses, my wandering hands
forbidden to touch
the lid, to sample
collective halitosis and rot.
Unmalleable, the enamel corpses inside
Dad's reliquary clung, until stripped,
to the gold, that gleaming
shapeshifter which, possessing all the time
in the world, awaited
its next future.

The Closest

to children of their own were me (nephew) and a stunted
grapefruit he'd raised from his breakfast

leftovers, nurtured with post-
drink ice cubes enhanced by whatever

sun found its way to their only window
sill, where my spindly

two-foot-tall elder sib
absorbed, across the seat of Uncle Jay's

armchair, opera or football oozing from a plastic-
cased Zenith radio. Their entire

domicile: one stuffed room—large bed, repro
colonial tallboy, expanding

table, etceteras, kitchenette—which they managed
on my aunt's buyer's pay from Gimbels,

while tracking the upward
creep of Uncle's margined

brokerage account until, just shy
of a mythic million, it collapsed. Fifteen years

younger, quiet, refined, she wanted kids but
listened to him and tolerated the abortions, while continuing

to extract tiptop entrees
and desserts from a miniature

stove. Everything transpired
in an upscale ocean-linerish hotel, where dozens

of deck chairs on its roof commanded the river's great
gray palisades—plus a cage for hitting golf balls. Though he never

endowed me with an authoritative
swing, I could balance thanks

to him on a bike. After
my potted brother took a twelve-story dive

down the light well, I was promoted
to #1 in Jay's

unreflective mind, Clara's
seething heart.

Big Museum

The world's greatest bird stuffer,
my boss, was a childless
Curator Emeritus, with no one
left to mentor except
fresh-from-high-school me,
who had hoped for a summer job in Mammals
or Bugs, but settled for cataloguing
with brass-nibbed pen and India ink
the sixteen-hundred-and-seventy-two
field labels hung on the dried-out legs
of Dr. C's ultimate
Belgian Congo collection, then
printing, teeny-tiny, officially-
numbered duplicate tags to flap
beside the originals. By winter,

part-timing just on Saturdays,
and alone, I learned to appreciate
his artistry, through handling
long strings of 1890's European sparrows
shackled at the feet.
Dusty, contorted,
crushed, seemingly, in gutters, beneath
the wheels of hell's brewery truck. Horribly
unlike the master's skins—equatorial
peacocks, honey-eaters,
weavers, immaculately sculpted
and plumped-out with cotton spooled on
the only perfect wand, an African

porcupine quill—eternally
dozing in fire-proof trays, tucked
shoulder-to-shoulder,
preened. He'd intended

to transmit all, instructing me, his last
hope for a successor, as he ignored
my metamorphosis into
an English major. **Step One**, Corpse
Acquisition, simplicity itself, he fantasized,
despite urban laws against gunning
down birds. *Look*, he commanded,
under the viaduct, where starlings
roost (where the diseased ones
fall). I found
nothing, during a rainy, guano-dripping dusk.
The kid's a liar, he assumed, and stomped
back to his office, same routine as when,
several times a day, he figured out
I couldn't get his Latin jokes. Were he a lesser
man he'd have flunked
and (thank God!) expelled me. Lesser
men, insensible to road kill, wouldn't
deviate from their commute, snag
from the shoulder and schlep to work
a bloated seagull ripened
in the heat. **Step**

32

Two: On a room-length work bench
beneath tall windows overlooking
Central Park, The Dissectionist Deploys
His Implements—scalpels, scissors, clamps,
cloths, touch-up brushes, thread
for suturing, needles, insecticide,
cornmeal, which absorbs secretions.
Step Three, Removing
Its Innards—everything soft
or skeletal—totally
a matter of technique. I watch
the chief incise ventrally, sternum
to pelvis, standing first beside
his shoulder, then gradually driven further
back, daunted by outgassing
from our sewage-eating volunteer, and settle
in the corridor, beyond practical
viewing range, the worst
smell ever becoming just
a memory.

        Step Four, Filling the Cavity,
Sewing Up, Making the Critter Look
Nice—largely unseen due to cringing
embarrassment at my wimpiness: Sorry,
O Great Iron Nosed
Explorers Club Member, generous
sharer of his anecdote on harvesting
the unique specimen of a presumably
extinct species: *One morning*

I'm walking along a trail beside Lake Kivu,
and there's a bird I've never seen before, so
I shoot it. Sorry, Discoverer
Many Moons Deceased, who invited me
to contemplate that small red cadaver,
and for the lack of your company when snow
whipped around the Planetarium roof.

Sorry I never fit,
taxonomically, any niche
carved by multiple would-be dads. It might
have cheered them up, cheered
me, too, eventually, with a spot
definitively secure
in the working museum's reference
library of skins, each entry filed
among its kind, sheltered by
floor-to-ceiling cabinets—covetable
nesting sites because here
and in former colonies everywhere
forests keep vanishing.

Irish Landscape with Spouse

A good disposition
has taken the hotel's
seventeen-year-old spaniel
quite some distance,
presently out to the bench
at the head of a little
cement dock,
to the woman in her blue
sweater, who dislikes
canines for their noxious
odors, unappetizing
hair, servility,
barking, snappishness,
who has been studying her maps,

gazing seaward along
the rock-bound cove.

His legs work poorly,
making the dog bounce
and wriggle, though he can move
fast enough. A matted
brown-and-white coat,
and the red growth
under his right eye
don't help, nor
do creaky moans beseeching
love. The morning deliciously quiet,
a sailboat slightly turning
around its mooring,

she so prefers cats but
pets him anyhow.

Hell Hath No Windows

no bird flight, no unfettered clouds,
     but it compensates with fluorescent, steel-
trussed cathedral ceilings, aisle
     upon aisle of hardware shelving: At 8:15,
Saturday's A.M., cubscoutmasters
     badger boys of seven and eight toward
virtue and a mini-seminar in craftsmanship,
     while parents trail after, few as disoriented
as I, who at nine wrestled miserably
     with himself over his irritated, stooping
father's bald head, an all-thumbs boobchild
     stuck holding the inventor's hammer
so Dad could fiddle, meticuously slow—*Give*
     him a whack and end it all, counselled
my demon of despair—in that bad
     memory of what might have been, now
just one more floater in my uninitiated
     eye, among distortions triggered
by labels and the wiles packaging works
     on ignorance—sex, violence, visions
as grabby as the grunge component
     of a Medieval altar piece, some
merely weird—*plate joining biscuits, air*
     chisel, anti spatter, self-centering
brad set—others twisted—*grinding*
     point tree, jitterbug sander, stud
finders loitering beside *The Aggressor,*
     bastard files, deep-throat
c-clamp—a witches' sabbath climaxed

by malpractice—*magnetic power
nut driver, Freud Circular Saw
Blades—50 teeth*—torment, not
temptation, not yummy, windowless
Las Vegas, where, nephew of a handsome
gambler, I once locked my rare
winnings in a box till checkout, thereby
tying myself to the mast, action
singing glitzy in my ears and rubbing at my party-
animal crotch; no,
clipboard in hand, I'm in narrow aisles, taking
names on the home turf of busy
gnomes, my purpose, exorcism (hardly
the wish list several fellow dads imagine),
and serving out my time, till noon, when
I'll sweep past the registers empty-
handed, without even a telescoping-
pole bulb changer, every last
pomegranate seed, unconsumed.

Thruway Blizzards, 1968-9

NY City/Buffalo

This used shitbrown Mercury Meteor contains girlfriend,
yours truly, and our pet parrot. 150 miles north
of Manhattan, a cold, clear day, most of the aftermath
snow scraped into shoulder berms, we're worried. The bird's
apathetic, irritable when awake, feathers dull, ditto
eyes. Dealer'd assured us it's a youthful yellowhead, well
worth our C note, only moulting.

How could he, mere
Kommandant of a Lower East Side reptile and avian
concentration camp, perceive that sweet, simpleminded,
charitable Typhoon had sacrificed himself by swapping livers
with a cirrhotic merchant-mariner? The car, which I believed
also possesed a bombproof provenance, in sympathy
with Typhoon was sputtering. My father insisted, thanks

to a busybody's stale tip, we must snap it up
from a bedraggled gas station in Queens, and he didn't realize
an ex-con several life-terms yet from going straight
was the new proprietor. Like my bird that Merc
had a rolled-back odometer, moved reluctantly, and coughed.
On his deathbed—macadam covered with sheets of crisp,
compacted icy snow—

Meteor san, kamikaziing out
his miserable destiny, blows a cylinder, oil spattering
the windshield. The heap chatters, heaves, its cabin fills
with gasses, the sort my owner's handbook advocates for parrot
euthanasia: Ventilate, stupid! Roll down window. Apply
antidote—oops, frigid air. See tropical sailor wafted
straight to cryonic shock. I'm 24, and want to die.

2.

Buffalo/Rochester RT

Dusk subsides in snow. Sporting a motor too powerful
for its frame and engine mounts, my poop-hued sucessor
Chevy Nova, palmed off cheap by the dermatologist dad
of a dubious childhood friend, vibrates alarmingly over
fifty-five. In the diffused, reflected, gustblown shine
of headlights it's hard to see, let alone pass, semis,
with their eccentric winds attacking larger winds, savage
eddies, sloughing us off to leeward.

                              Everybody parties:
shotgun rides our revered teach; his claque
of students stuff the back. We wallow like a piled-high
garbage scow. *I'm losing my buzz,* whimpers the mentor,
through his grizzled mustache, through his dishevelled, mumbled,
ill-attended book signing, then from car to bar to bar until
the 2 AM close, and again a maelstrom. We race
upstate, massaged by the lilt of Gaelic pipes—*I've lost
my buzz*—as if a sober transit were utter calamity.

3.

NY City/Buffalo

Next winter, same girlfriend, same overjuiced
monster, balder tires, low on gas, beautifulest
nightstorm, windless but exceptionally cold, a quiet
stretch of oceanic spaces between towns, sparse
traffic, less and less. Crystalline waves accumulate
and suggest love, rapture of the snowy deep, our rare,
relaxed intimacy a disarming gift from shaggy-maned
boreal gods smiling down into our cushioned
potently heated obscurity.
                    When the fuel
gauge redlines we spot a service island rising
on our left, churn up to it, park among heavily-mounded
comradely vehicles, then knee-high in glitter break
trail toward a crowded cafeteria, where angry cops
demand we justify why the devil we were out there,
the Thruway shut for hours, with more than one bogged-
down tank-dry lost soul already stiff as ice.

Formerly Candlestick Park: Un-Zen Koan

A large Toro's tidal sound
reflected off 55,000 empty seats
waxes, wanes as the mower
circles home plate clockwise
heading up the left field line, turns
and paces the ground crew's
solitary hoseman towards a fresh bib
in right center, where his benign
wetting of the warning track
resumes. August 1: midseason

dying from old age, Giants
on the road, the afternoon sun
flooding over my shoulder
like a well-trained reading lamp.
Limitless sky, just the place twinkling
popups love to disappear, ascends
beyond the light stanchions. Seems
any minute the glacially
slow preamble to a game-
winning grand slam. Any minute
an accretion of bleeders, muffs, and bad
hops tailor made to leave me
a nasty hangover. Me, the only one
sitting in the stands, a lonely oxymoron,
Stadium Man, compound
of ancestor worship and future
excitation, monumentally adept at the traditional

baseball thing—waiting—while officials
print my Pennant Race
Plan tickets, which guarantee
playoff admission rights contingent
on the *if* of squeaking
past L.A. thanks
to yesterday's dramatic
deadline acquisition: three better-
than-average pitchers joining
the team in Cincinnati. It's always

waiting: for garlic fries or
a catcher with power, for the line
drive to hook foul, for an out-
of-options rookie to clear
waivers, for the injury
report, the end of a rain
delay, for next year. Eliminate
the waiting, and what's
left? One
hand clapping in the emptyish
forest when the ash
tree, destined
mother of Louisville
Sluggers, that
sonorous
fat lady
falls.

Ballplayer

Noon Approaching, South San Francisco

He's an entering freshman on a patched-
together outfit of bigger stronger veterans, fielded
for summer training by two small private
high schools. They are overmatched opposing
the far bigger stronger JV of an enormous
public, perennial city-championship contender.
With the game nearly finished and well
beyond reach he's finally sent in, two outs,
two on via a walk and a plunking. The pitcher's
a head taller, his velocity in the sixties.
Couple of swings, no contest.
The rookie takes a pair, fouls off
the next, takes again. Now,
the count full, he fouls one straight back,
right on it, barely missed.
The fatal pitch is high and away,
borderline at best. He lays off and gets rung up
by an umpire probably thinking lunch.

Late Afternoon, Nicasio

Outfield decaying to brown stubble seamed
with parched dirt. Throwing off
a Little League mound, post-
season, I'm grateful
if only from a dozen short yards

I can still locate the plate, grateful
for getting hit. Nearly everything
comes back as line drives and sharp
grounders up the middle or pulled
to left, maybe thumps the adverts
on a waist-high fence or rattles
its chain links, occasionally hops
over them. Sweating hard,
I'm delighted till it dawns that the batter,
despite racking up a personal best, has sunk,
as my pitch count approaches 90,
into desperation
while my geriatric arm starts heading
south, along with his objective—just one
home run. He faces

me on this miniature diamond,
a bagload of balls sprawled at my feet,
an aging 14-year-old eager to break in
his expensive just-bought longer, heavier,
metal bat, determined—
after Bonds launched two last night—
he'll finally put one out. He knows
someday, without question, also knows
someday may come too late.

                         His official
fences moved back,
his original teammates, five-
to-eights who collected their trophies
as bribes for showing up, stopped

showing up, and the residual
merely adequate LL Majors seemed
to retire at twelve, adopting
golf or tennis. But he,
cursed by love and will
to defy probabilities, with a hopeless gene pool—
no hand-me-down chops, no
Alou family connection to toss him
apprenticeships, not even a respectable
incentive—say escape from the Dominican
slums—my kid clings
to a roster spot on ever-
more-potent teams. His bat

authentically keeps going
crack, the balls *thud*
or *jingle* against the fence, yet nothing
impacts on the fly, let alone sails
beyond. My arm hurting quite awhile,
the boy at the plate resists quitting.
We argue. I return to my car and sulk.
He hits fungos but eventually recollects:
The video rental closes at seven.

Daybreak, New Year's, 1993

Such dull luxury here
for contemplating my boys, who
collusively accept
Santa, with superior
six-year-old wisdom.

The wet portal to our next
millennium opens
a crack further, smoke
rising tentatively.

In the living room one coughs,
lingering, chesty, to ignite
my dread of medical
bureaucracy and sticky refrigerated
bottles that echo
greater dreads—

resistant TB bap bap
for the fiscally incompetent;
zing! AIDS
for the naughty; trendy
from rainforests, those wild
assonant hemoragic
fevers: Marburg,
Ebola boom
boom boom, lumps
of coal for humanity
at large.

No drought now

of inspiration to banish
ennui. My telephone
rings. Perhaps
the sun, tra la,
trying to get through.

What People Earn

"What People Earn"
(Cover Story from *Parade*, 3/13/'05)

Although among these 137 inch-
square faces, places, ages, occupations,
incomes, it's weirdly gratifying
to read Sponge Bob, "ageless,"
raked in $1.2 billion—Kudos,
SB—Katie Clark, 21, a North
Vegas danceuse (body not shown) couldn't
crack thirty thou. Call that
earning? Annualized, how much
are you worth? Idaho archaeologist
Steve Armstrong, 40, says
53 grand; Christopher Ivy, age 51, highway
maintenance of Belleville, IL 29, whereas
Teresa Dougherty, a bravely-smiling New
Jersey school-bus driver, tallies 26. One
of my favorites, the spunky LA
actress Renee Zellweger, only racks up
21, just kidding, million.

How about that, tow-boat captain

Tom Miller, 40, Ponce de Leon, Fla, sitting
on a squalid 85, or you, Fresno Mike
McKneely, 30, deputy DA, 51 large—Where's
the justice?—after stuffing scads of scumbags
into cells? Alfred Cocina busts his ass
running an Hawaiian coffee company to realize
50. Al can't hardly afford pineapple pupus
at the Wiki Wok. And Yevgenia C, layaway
clerk up by Fairbanks, AK, good for a cool

17.5, should try loving the real estate racket.
Clue her in, M. B. Gourlay, Wilmington, Delaware,
mortgage financier, who pulled 280,000
little green ones out of her hat, while Gualberto
Medina, Jersey broker, trundled home
a jolly 600 Benjamins times ten.

Feeling prime NG, Pittsburgh secretary,

about your 23? Or you, Tracy
Gregory, environmental tech, gleaning
a measly 28, did you squeeze yourself
dry as Sponge Bob? Sweat blood
like Angeleno Lindsay Lohan, 18,
over her ten mil? No way. Not unless
you've stared yourself in the eye and commanded
you measure up, rock, kick butt,
cut mustard, put your shoulder to the wheel,
suck in your gut and salute for 65, such as
Zach R, 36, US Army Specialist First Class,
who all must trust remains alive,
a success in itself.

Stakes

During the middle game
he apologizes,

sticks an empty
Gatorade bottle under

our cement chess table, pees
and empties it

behind his shoulder
into a public flower bed.

I'm thinking,
Missing teeth, smelly: this is

one broken-down hustler.
But distracted trying

to avoid personal embarrassment—lack
of practice has me hearing

footsteps, seeing ghosts all
over the board—I never

guess the opposition might
be wetting himself because of that

fiver I don't need
and can anybody say whether

he even owns one
to pay me off.

Who Knows

if a dead man cares
whether he gets paid
in women or dried grapes,
if he can tell the difference when

he makes it to Paradise,
whole again from his holy
explosion, heart aflame for his
compensatory virgins, his
houris, and trips over a dagger
in the Koran, beside *hur*,
directing him to the small
print, the footnoted
Aramaic fundamentals: *an adjective*
in the feminine plural meaning
simply "white." If

he bothers to read
further will he find
peace upon learning
Paradise referred to *a garden*
of flowing waters, abundant
fruits and... hur, *a prized*
delicacy in the ancient Near East—
"white raisins" of crystal
clarity. Here,

on earth, this haven
of belief, there's always something worth
fighting for, something
to sink your teeth into.

The Annual So-Called "Hunting Trip"
Montana, September Twenty-two, Two Thousand and One

Late afternoon, the mountain—
having retracted its bears,
as well as its legendary elk—
retains only a little anger for the creek
to carry away. Unscrupulous
flies have discovered
the abundant horse
apples of our campsite. We reject
their partnership offers the way
the sun rejects
winter—as long as we can.

A rancher told me
every aspen grove,
no matter how large, consists
of sprouts off underground
latticework stemming from
an ancestral tree,
decayed maybe thousands
of years ago. What if
you dismount and discover
yourself pissing on a delicate
sapling? Don't worry
your sprinkles may poison
puny roots, but its descendants
will bear an immortal
grudge. The grasses

seem more plentiful this year, the blue
grouse as ignorantly self-confident as always

in the low branches of stunted
aspen, determined
to behave like nothing
taller than a coyote could threaten
them.

　　　With extreme prejudice, summer
got terminated in New York, unofficially, ten
days ahead of schedule. Now
we four men having flown
up to the Beaverhead
National Forest, ride,
drink, roost and pretend
nothing special is after
us or our babies.
Yesterday we left the bows
idling at camp, but carried cell phones
high onto the ridge,
to hunt
for a strong
signal.

April, 2003: It's All Over But

the shooting, the throatcutting, the poisoning,
the interrogations, show trials, imprisonments,
the physical rehabilitations, prostheses,
the infrastructure upgrades,
the profiteering, the quislings, the factions,
the propaganda, the stage-managed elections,
the boundary disputes, vendettas,
assassinations, suicidebombings,
indifference, neglect, abandonment,
all over today, all over Iraq.

The Girl with the Leash

doesn't appear to worry much
about its other end. Fun-loving, power-
mad, a thoughtlessly
vindictive woman of action, the perfect
Abu Ghraib patsy. Already
an irresistible wave of
retribution gathers behind her
back, curling above her bobbed

head. Her leash, poor child,
connects to the nearly-wriggled-
out pin of a fragmentation
grenade. The brass
will use her body as a hand
towel, shred it like paper
wiping themselves
clean on her fatigues.

If she *were* paper I
would write upon her
atrocity photo my
implausible disavowals, my
poems of innocence.

Here under her left nipple,
and again across her smooth-shaven
mons Veneris, I would inscribe
anti-war protests, my solidarity
with the oppressed. Poet,

not a shooter of rifles,
I do what I can with the time
at my disposal. But we

are attached, possessing
and possessed,
my mistress,
my bitch.

Busman's Holiday, Cloudy

Back against a rock, legs
flat on the sand, I listen
to the sociopathic sea
grumble. Incoherent
and demented from swallowing
garbage. No guilt
for the engulfments,
kidnappings, battery—no more
than Bonaparte, beached
at St. Helena. Can I tolerate
a patient who's never
been innocent, just oblivious?
If it knew to care, it might
protest,

> *I've given birth, played,*
> *when in the mood, kept*
> *secrets, donated food. I'm*
> *unprejudiced, no Hitler.*

This damned
ocean resembles a flasher
dumped on me at community
mental health. Kicked
out of jail—old,
scuzzy, illiterate—his pleasures
booze and *waving.* Condemned
to psychotherapy, blank,
contemptuous, he treated
me like an idiot. Eventually

I wised up. We agreed
until I could hand him
off, our sessions were just
running out the clock.

Piglet Mind

Romances

For X: Res Casino Weekend

Three years no poems—living
outside myself but not
outdoors. Now

on this balcony, sunset
just finished, still
a little duck noise
to party up the lake,
nobody who wants any-
thing around, *and,* in my shirt
pocket, coupons, each good
for a Margarita,

        I'll cut
you cards,
      Li Po,
          for that
              quarter moon.

For Y: Worry-free Day

no more mountains visible
from this plateau so high the world drops
away at the edges leaving
supple yellow grass in motion
a single horse that seems to gallop off
in all directions

For Zoe

you must be learning a lot
up there in the woods
from your favorite kinds of snow
bad luck bad weather welcoming
big fears

what spaciousness you offer
an absence of questions not
cold but open possibility
like realizing the trees won't mind
my talk my silence

Handsome is as
handsome does, we cubes
often remark. We never
lie. Why bother? Cubes
have no secrets, except, maybe,
how we reproduce.

When we wish, it's for
a little holiday
in Cuba. They speak
our language there and it's
sunny despite the embar-
go

Did you hear the one
about the two
cubes? The three? The cube
that ran into an oval?
They're all good,
and all the same.

BECUBE
BECUBE
BECUBE
BECUBE

We're really into
relationships, we cubes,
getting along by going
along or staying put—
whatever causes less
friction.

Cubes make excellent
friends for hysterics,
hypertensives. We calm them
down. Even better friends for
autistic children rocking
rhythmically on a string.

Thanks for listening, for
caring, for lending
your time. It's so
cubelike of you, to give
quietly, as if
you were hardly there.

Language Fallen into the Wrong Hands

Someone's small child may say
fidgeder, inducing a low-level
buzz; eventually, with
luck and application,
refrigerator—the radical
power surge of a word
that commands respect.

Crimes ensue from grasping
after impact, clutching
beyond knowledge, beyond
merit. At seven, he signs
his homework *"Simon Fuck."*

Upon Encountering Ovid's *No lyres for this lot, no poetry.*

for Charles Martin, translator
Metamorphoses, Book XII

If there's one thing Augustus really knows,
from long practice, it's how to hurt a guy. Death?
a minor penalty, fellow Roman, reserved
for misdemeanors, but honorable death's
a veritable reward. Dedicated screwoffs
earn slavery—for their entire families—plus
galling confiscations, while we namby-
pamby city boys rate banishment

from The Urbs. Back to nature, Jove forbid, goes
our belaurelled disrespecter of deities and Emperors alike.
Let's see how he appreciates the companionship
of illiterates, boors, and those loser animals,
plants, waters, rocks, formerly human,
debased by angry gods, or gods—this *slays* me—
gods who pitied them. Was it in the library or at the resort
Ovid first made their distant acquaintance?

Now may he enjoy, breathlessly close-up, salacious
gossip with a brown recluse spider, rant with an ant
at the intimate mirthful twitterings of established
birdbrains. By all means let him live, transformed
to beseech from The Almighty, how *droll,*
his reenlargement, his second chance, echoing
Echo: a voice, a voice, and nothing
more.

Relative Unknowns

For Jerry Kilbride

Propriety

Don't bewail Shiko (1665-1731),
that *shamelessly ambitious* haiku poet
whose personality defect Blyth believes
cost him pals. But hurt his chances?
Tolerated by Basho, he fathered
an enormous number of books,...[and]
his own [durable, trademark] *school*
in Mino, abuzz with paper factories.

Are there unambitious poets? No.
Not even the reclusive, virginal Emily
D (1829-1886). Avoidant?
You betcha—though totally avid.
Em, a superficially decent girl, tampered
with her ulterior motives, ceased
to submit. Her wheelless carriage
brought, eventually, not even pals.

2.

Constraint

Preferably, life slowly erodes like
lying on a neatly-made bed,
back aching just a little, petting the old cat
before our nap. Yesterday I read

with amusement about Bokudo,
an 18th Century sword-sharpener and writer
whose *favorite subject was drowsiness.*
His fame stems from a single haiku

concerning new leaves of a spring morning.
It concludes, *no wonder I'm sleepy.*
My buddy laughed also, but pointed
out that Bokudo couldn't nod off,

given his job, during long hours at work,
and expect to keep all his fingers. Two weeks ago,
gazing toward trees, I sliced
my thumb, cleaning a pocket knife.

3.

Her Reputation Burgeoned Posthumously

Just past my 54th birthday I realized, worse
fates exist than having once resembled a gifted child
who lacked follow-through. After all, I never
died insane at the end of World War II,

the way Hisajo, age 55,
did, dishonored, struck from the official
register, her book unpublished, *many enemies,...*
no friends, at home and abroad.

Fallen leader of a coterie of female poets,
passionate,...always in love with somebody,...only one
thought in mind.

Moonlight pierces
her *thin clothes/ to the very skin.* Immensely
sensitive about herself, she might savage

a clumsy hairdresser. *Kawazu* (frog) spears
tombo (dragonfly). *Wa kata ka* (Got it?):
Ah, Hisajo! Your pen name—*Eternal Woman.*

Note: Italicized quotations are from R. H. Blyth's *A History of Haiku*
(Tokyo, The Hokuseido Press, 1963).

Consolation

for Nancy Keane

Seeing the famous poet on his way to dinner stop in plain view
to urinate against a tree, an editor, my slight acquaintance,
expressed outrage. I felt grateful he never caught me
marking territory, felt doubly grateful for my bond with the leaky,
creaky bard, while nonetheless downhearted
about expectations, standards, those responsibilities
of public life—the uncharitableness. And grateful I'd escaped
notice, for everything, I felt, that remains
between me and the unheralded tree.

Rural Diptych

A Son of Adam, Only Nominally

Cold morning, the absolute damp
stillness of air. Sun
designates the north
side of the drainage,
the tall bare creek alder, the young
oak's top, the bishop
pines, unkempt
laurels, while shade categorizes the apples,
rhododendrons and grass: all this
nameable but so? Labels
ignorantly bestowed, indifferently carried.

When I ponder
the neighbor's roof blanched
like my comatose lawn, who cares
whether I'm absorbed by
dew or frost?

2.

Noticeable from the Lawn

The long-gone tenant,
slight, romantic, subtly
beautiful, had always seemed depressed
between boyfriends. One of whom,
a housepainter, superimposed
a red heart on the white
arch curving over the porch
steps. They broke up.

                    Years ago
she moved. His love-
cartoon survives, even in this
time of thieves and fanatics. Has she

a boyfriend now? Has he
a heart?

Piglet Mind

I confess
I'm still
a very little person, not
only when lying
on my back beneath a clear
night sky I fall up to
where there's no identity,
but right inside my skin, as *I*
slow-trot past obsolete
factories, along degraded
arteries jammed with dull,
oblivious corpuscles. When new,

I could find *me*
in smaller yet, yets such as
bugs destroyed
by my curiosity,
playing their doctor, or hypo-
chondriacal mom. I got

ambitious to grow
a big-guy's chest for bursting
forth from this ditsy
homunculus but shirked
the calisthenics. Large women
frightened me; others
required protection. Scholarship,
a trainride through suburbs,
shrank everything.
That's about it.

Lucky I live near oaks.
In my acorn trust fund
I root,
toot, and scribble
with my snoot.
Embrace your insignificance!
Thus saith I, Piglet,
(just to myself).

Epilogue

Twins Discuss Heaven

Real or not?
It's open-

sunroof weather and
traffic's creeping,
but at least we aren't late
for kindergarten. Politely,
from the back seat, Simon
asks my opinion.

*I don't
think so.*

Taking his turn
at shotgun, George,
emphatic: *I believe
in outer space. There isn't
room for heaven.*

Last week he pulled up
Teacher's skirt.

Simon elaborates.
*We would see
Grandpa Seymour flying around
in his coffin.* He knows
we all go

underground, boxed
and fully animate. That

settles it. Now Si wants
singing from the radio, as
we inch
ourselves along.